RELATIONSHIP   MONEY

TIME

WANTING WHAT YOU WANT

Thanks to the Creative Team:

JR

Susan Austin

Kerri Morrison

Hamish MacDonald

Shannon Waller

Jennifer Bhatthal

Lynda Buwalda

Paul Hamilton

Christine Nishino

TM & © 2015. The Strategic Coach Inc. All rights reserved. No part of this work may be reproduced in any form, or by any means whatsoever, without written permission from The Strategic Coach Inc., except in the case of brief quotations embodied in critical articles and reviews.

Strategic Coach®, Strategic Coach® Program, Unique Ability®, and Impact Filter™ are trademarks of The Strategic Coach Inc.

Illustrations by Hamish MacDonald.

Printed in Toronto, Canada. The Strategic Coach Inc., 33 Fraser Avenue, Suite 201, Toronto, Ontario, M6K 3J9.

This publication is meant to strengthen your common sense, not to substitute for it. It is also not a substitute for the advice of your doctor, lawyer, accountant, or any of your advisors, personal or professional.

If you would like further information about the Strategic Coach® Program or other Strategic Coach® services and products, please telephone 416.531.7399 or 1.800.387.3206.

Library and Archives Canada Cataloguing in Publication

Sullivan, Dan, 1944-, author
    Wanting what you want / Dan Sullivan.

ISBN 978-1-897239-39-1 (pbk.)

    1. Self-actualization (Psychology). I. Title.

BF637.S4S86785 2015   158.1   C2015-901291-0

Contents

Introduction	6
Chapter 1 **Wanting vs. Needing**	10
Chapter 2 **Wanting Bypasses Politics**	18
Chapter 3 **Transformation: Gaining The Capability**	24
Chapter 4 **Letting Go Of "Giving Back"**	30
Chapter 5 **The Four Freedoms**	36
Chapter 6 **Wanting Is About Cooperation**	42
Chapter 7 **Wanting Is Energizing**	48
Chapter 8 **Wanting Is Rewarding**	54
Conclusion **A Lifetime State Of Play**	60
The Strategic Coach Program **Expanding Entrepreneurial Freedom**	66

Introduction

On August 15, 1978, when I was 34 years old, I was both divorced and bankrupt on the same day. I was divorced in the morning and bankrupt later that afternoon. It was like getting two really bad report cards on the same day, and I was looking at big failures in two parts of my life. During the next three or four months, I had a strong feeling that how I handled these two situations was going to determine what the rest of my life looked like. As a result, I made two distinct decisions.

Number one, I was going to free everybody else from any responsibility for my present situation. I decided that nobody else was responsible for what happened to me, except me—which, it turns out, was actually very liberating because I got to take back my power over the situation. When you blame somebody else, you've given power to the other person. I decided I needed my power back.

Second, I decided that I was in that situation because I wasn't telling myself what I really wanted. So I set a goal that I would start a journal, and every day I would write something in the journal about what I wanted in the current situation. The only requirement was that I had to write down at least one sentence about what I wanted, and I had to use the word *want*.

I wasn't telling myself what I wanted.
You see, back then I figured out that the reason I was divorced was because I was expecting someone else to provide me with something. Why did I go bankrupt? I was expecting someone else to guarantee my success. So I stopped and realized I wasn't actually telling myself what I really wanted.

Wanting What You Want

AUGUST 15, 1978

TWO "REPORT CARDS" THAT *CHANGED MY LIFE*:

DIVORCED!

BANKRUPT!

DECISION 1

"I FREE EVERYONE ELSE FROM *RESPONSIBILITY FOR MY SITUATION*."

DECISION 2

"FOR THE NEXT 25 YEARS, I WILL KEEP A DAILY JOURNAL OF *WHAT I WANT*."

ALL BUT 12 DAYS = 9,119 WANTS!

THE 25-YEAR DISCOVERY!

THERE'S A HUGE DIFFERENCE BETWEEN **NEEDING & WANTING**

WANTING WHAT YOU WANT —*WITHOUT JUSTIFICATION*...

FREES YOUR *FUTURE* FROM YOUR *PAST*.

Introduction

I made it a goal to write in that journal every day for 25 years. I believed if I did so, I was going to get really good at wanting. I started right at the end of 1978, and on New Year's Eve 2003, the end of the 25 years, I went out to dinner with two close friends and my wife, Babs, who, by the way, happened to be one of the things written down in that journal that I really wanted. I told them, "Today I've reached a milestone. I've completed a project. Every day, except for 12 (out of 9,131), during the last 25 years, I've done this exercise of writing down what I want. Twenty-five years later, I can tell you I'm a really powerful wanter."

25 years of practice made me a great "wanter."

It was this experience of wanting, wanting, wanting that caused me to see the very sharp difference between wanting and needing. My divorce and bankruptcy in 1978 had been the result of needing others to be responsible for my progress and well being. But when I switched from needing to wanting, I quickly freed myself from the negative memories and emotions related to these experiences. And as my day by day wanting increased over the 25 years, it became clear that I could also free myself from other failures and frustrations in my past.

What I noticed as I wrote down my wants in my journal was that I wasn't writing down any justification for what I wanted or why I wanted it. So I got a 25-year experience of wanting without justification. From that, I noticed the incredible freedom I obtained out of developing my brain in just this one direction. I liberated myself.

Wanting because they want it. No justification.

Now, because I'm so sure of the payoff from this wanting, I'm creating coaching structures and tools for successful entrepreneurs in my Strategic Coach® Program to allow them to make the same journey to a breakthrough that I did. They can make it much more quickly than I did because I can show them that this is the payoff.

What I've discovered from my 40 years of coaching entrepreneurs is that the most successful individuals are those who are very skillful in "wanting what they want." The more they want what they want—because they want it—the more successful they become. And the less they justify what they want, the more liberated they become.

Making your future the authority over today.

We are all creatures who live with a sense of time consisting of past, present, and future. But we are unequal in our mastery of these three time dimensions. Many people's lives are increasingly controlled by their pasts. As they get older, they are only capable of repeating what they've already learned and achieved. As they get older, every new possibility that they think about is undermined by their need to justify it to other people and their past. But there is another, much better way of organizing your thinking and action in your daily life. In this superior approach, you increasingly make the future the authority over what you do in your daily life. And as you become increasingly skillful at leading a future-based life, it is your past that has to justify itself to your future.

The liberating skill of Wanting What You Want.

The best way of describing this future-creating skill is Wanting What You Want. And the single most important thing to understand about this "wanting" skill is that the reason you want something is because you want it. Period.

Chapter 1:
Wanting vs. Needing

What distinguishes the top 1 percent of the world's entrepreneurs from the other 99 percent?

The big thing I've noticed from coaching entrepreneurs for over 40 years is a real dividing line between extremely successful entrepreneurs and those who peak after reaching a certain level of success. The dividing line seems to consist of two words: *needing* and *wanting*.

There are the vast majority of entrepreneurs who are as successful as they need to be, and then there's an elite group of entrepreneurs who grow and grow and grow with no apparent ceiling. The difference I've noticed from studying these two groups extensively is that the second group of entrepreneurs is as successful as they *want* to be.

Those who stop and those who always grow.
When you're as successful as you need to be, there's a stopping point you reach when you've satisfied your needs. It's unconscious, of course, so the entrepreneur won't even notice it happening. But when you're as successful as you want to be, you just keep growing and expanding. This is because the moment you reach one level of wanting, there is another just beyond that. I began to see this distinction make a huge difference between people who get to a certain level and stop and the other entrepreneurs who keep growing all their lives. It all comes down to the difference between needing and wanting.

The psychologist Abraham Maslow created his famous pyramid of needs more than 70 years ago. In Maslow's hier-

Wanting What You Want

archy, there are five levels of needs: Survival, Safety, Belonging, Esteem, and Self-Actualization.

These five levels implicitly ask this question: "Are you everything you could be?" This suggests there's a "perfect you" — an idealized version of yourself that is based on other people's judgment of what you should be.

But what about wants? The payoff for wanting is not self-actualization but rather self-transformation. From this perspective, you can picture yourself becoming something that is bigger and better. You don't need to reach some "perfect you." You're a self-transformer who keeps making your future bigger and better by wanting a life of expanded freedom.

I have found there to be four key differences between needers and wanters.

Difference 1: Internal vs. External

For one reason or another, "needers" are taking their directions from outside, external sources. They're being told, "You'll be successful if you do this," and they do this. Plus, they have certain necessities. They have to make a certain income for their family. They have to attain a certain position to establish themselves at a certain social level. More than likely, they're in an industry where there are rewards for being considered the top person. But, in every case, all the judgments and all the criteria about how successful they are come from an external source. Once they reach the top, once they satisfy their needs based on external criteria, there is nowhere further to go. They step off the gas pedal. They've reached the top, but this is strictly in the eyes of other people.

Wanting What You Want

THE NEEDERS (99%)

- ARE EXTERNALLY MOTIVATED
- SEEK SECURITY
- HAVE A SCARCITY MINDSET
- ARE REACTIVE

People who are as successful as they want to be are 100 percent internally driven, so all their goals and all the standards by which they're living their lives don't come from the outside—they actually come from the inside. Consequently, they don't pay much attention to external standards. They have a certain sense of what the next growth stage is for them. They have a certain sense of what constitutes a breakthrough for them, and, because of this, they're a constant surprise to the people who know them and work with them.

They always seem to be doing something that goes beyond what anyone else would need to do. Often, you notice this as they get older. It's almost as if at seventy, they're more ambitious than they were at fifty. Yet at fifty, they were more ambitious than they were at thirty. People who are externally driven have a sense that when you get to a certain level of success in life, you just maintain the status quo. But why would you want to stop growing?

Always experimenting, innovating, and creating.

For the elite group of entrepreneurs, growth is a lifelong activity, and up until they run out of life, they're continually experimenting, innovating, and creating new breakthroughs. It all comes because they're as successful as they want to be and not as successful as they need to be.

Many outside circumstances force you to need something, but no one can force you to want anything. Wanting is an independent motivation that comes totally from the inside. As an entrepreneur, you are not compelled from the outside to transform yourself and your company. You're entirely self-motivated to do it.

This independent act of wanting results in greater imagination, greater vision, and greater capabilities. This means that you never stay fixed at the highest levels of achievement. You're compelled from the inside to want a bigger and better future. As a result, you and your company keep expanding and growing. The more you act on your wants, the more you become independent of outside circumstances.

Difference 2: Freedom vs. Security

Needs relate to a sense of security, while wants relate to a sense of freedom. Everybody wants security, but not everybody wants freedom. For some people, security is enough. And, moreover, they expect their security to be supplied to them from the outside. It's an external thing. So they hold other people responsible for their security.

THE WANTERS (1%)

- ARE INTERNALLY MOTIVATED
- PURSUE FREEDOM
- HAVE AN ABUNDANCE ATTITUDE
- ARE CREATIVE

Entrepreneurs, however, desire freedom, and freedom is actually created from the inside.

Difference 3: Abundance vs. Scarcity

The reason why some people need security to be generated from the outside is because they live in a world of scarcity. In their world, there are only so many opportunities. There's only so much money. There's only so much time. There's only so much status. And so they know that there's a competitive quality about it, that you have to compete for security and to be taken care of by other people. This makes them very conscious of their security because they don't actually generate these things for themselves. They have to compete with other "needy" people for them.

Chapter 1

As much abundance as they want to create.
In western society, people compete for schooling. They compete for promotions. Anytime you get a scarce situation, you're immediately going to get competition. The entrepreneurial world, on the other hand, is very abundant. This is because you are operating in the realm of freedom, and it's generated from the inside. Your desire for freedom is not competing with anyone else's sense of freedom. The freedom is as abundant as you want to create it. It requires that you create it, but there is no limit on your ability to create freedom from the inside. This is a wonderfully different world with no competition because the freedom that you have in mind is not the freedom that somebody else has in mind.

This means you're not using up someone else's space. You're not using up someone else's position because, before it's created, it didn't even exist.

Difference 4: Creative vs. Reactive
The fourth distinction is that, in the needs world, you are reacting. You're continually in a reactive situation, which is especially true in our rapidly changing world.

Some of these changes are scientific, technological, economic, and political. And people are in a constant state of reactivity. So in a certain sense, people in the needing world are always playing defense. They're hoping that what they have can stay the same. But the new kinds of changes can happen in their workplace, and all of a sudden, they have to react, increasing their need for security.

In the realm of wanting, though, it's totally creative. You are literally taking things that no one really knows about and

THE WANTERS (1%)
- ARE INTERNALLY MOTIVATED
- PURSUE FREEDOM
- HAVE AN ABUNDANCE ATTITUDE
- ARE CREATIVE

Entrepreneurs, however, desire freedom, and freedom is actually created from the inside.

Difference 3: Abundance vs. Scarcity

The reason why some people need security to be generated from the outside is because they live in a world of scarcity. In their world, there are only so many opportunities. There's only so much money. There's only so much time. There's only so much status. And so they know that there's a competitive quality about it, that you have to compete for security and to be taken care of by other people. This makes them very conscious of their security because they don't actually generate these things for themselves. They have to compete with other "needy" people for them.

As much abundance as they want to create.

In western society, people compete for schooling. They compete for promotions. Anytime you get a scarce situation, you're immediately going to get competition. The entrepreneurial world, on the other hand, is very abundant. This is because you are operating in the realm of freedom, and it's generated from the inside. Your desire for freedom is not competing with anyone else's sense of freedom. The freedom is as abundant as you want to create it. It requires that you create it, but there is no limit on your ability to create freedom from the inside. This is a wonderfully different world with no competition because the freedom that you have in mind is not the freedom that somebody else has in mind.

This means you're not using up someone else's space. You're not using up someone else's position because, before it's created, it didn't even exist.

Difference 4: Creative vs. Reactive

The fourth distinction is that, in the needs world, you are reacting. You're continually in a reactive situation, which is especially true in our rapidly changing world.

Some of these changes are scientific, technological, economic, and political. And people are in a constant state of reactivity. So in a certain sense, people in the needing world are always playing defense. They're hoping that what they have can stay the same. But the new kinds of changes can happen in their workplace, and all of a sudden, they have to react, increasing their need for security.

In the realm of wanting, though, it's totally creative. You are literally taking things that no one really knows about and

WANTING IS *UNPREDICTABLE,* BECAUSE IT CREATES...

THINGS NOBODY KNOWS ABOUT

WAYS NOBODY THOUGHT OF BEFORE

RESULTS NOBODY CONSIDERED POSSIBLE

putting them together in a way that nobody had thought about before to produce a result that nobody knew could actually exist. And you can see this in the world around us, especially in the realm of new technologies.

We have many 21st-century role models of people who seem to have created new technological capabilities, resources, and opportunities almost out of thin air. One thing all of these innovators have in common is that they are not acting out of needing but out of wanting. They are internally-driven and focused on expanding their own personal freedom. They are the 1 percent entrepreneurs who operate in a world of growing abundance and who continually create bigger and better futures for themselves and everyone else.

Chapter 2:
Wanting Bypasses Politics

In the needs world, which is based on scarcity, anytime you get three or four human beings together, there are going to be political issues: *Who's getting what?* This happens very quickly because essentially people are competing for scarce resources: scarcity of recognition, scarcity of status, scarcity of opportunity. The general perception from the vast majority of people is that there's a scarcity of almost everything. Therefore, you have to have some mechanism for dealing with scarcity so that it doesn't result in open violence.

That's why political systems exist: to prevent violence due to the competition for scarce resources or what are perceived to be scarce resources. Whether it's just a few people or a whole country, if scarcity is the issue, then political competition, negotiation, bargaining, and compromise come into play.

Politics: Competing over scarcity.

The world of scarcity is frightfully competitive—so much so that the competition itself can use up most people's energy. There's not very much left over for fun. There's not very much left over for creativity. There's not a lot left over for cooperation because everybody's striving in a competitive framework where there is only so much opportunity, money, and time. In western society, people compete for education, popularity, influence, status, and power—all of which are scarce.

Anytime you get a scarce situation, you're immediately going to get competition. And those in the needing realm know that you have to compete for security and you have to compete to be taken care of by other people. And so they're

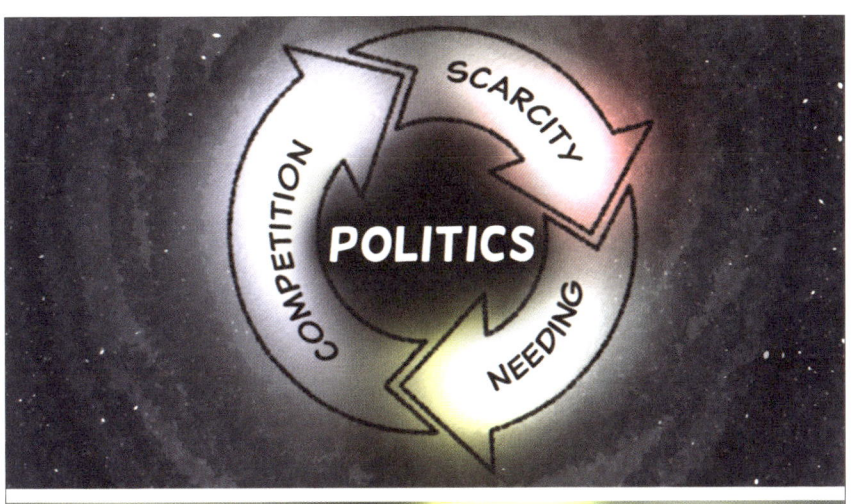

Wanting What You Want

SCARCITY → NEEDING → COMPETITION → **POLITICS**

IN THE WORLD OF *NEEDS*, EVERYONE HAS TO *COMPETE*... ...FOR *SCARCE RESOURCES*.

TIME
MONEY
STATUS
POWER
INFLUENCE
POPULARITY
OPPORTUNITY

BUT WANTING COMPLETELY *BYPASSES* THAT WORLD OF *CAPTIVITY & CHAOS*.

very conscious of their security because they don't actually generate these things for themselves. They have to compete and compromise with other people to get at least some of what they need.

Freedom from energy-draining competition.

Once you get into the world of abundance, however, there's no more scarcity and, therefore, no more competition. There's no more competing for capabilities, resources, and opportunities that you want. What this does is free everyone up from the energy-draining competition over scarcity, and the envy, disappointment, and feeling of failure that go along with it.

Now you're entering a world where new resources are being created all the time. In the world of wanting, no competition is really required.

Going back to the story of my divorce and bankruptcy that opened this book, it's clear to me now how I freed my life from both politics and competition with the two decisions I made. First, I relieved everyone else from the responsibility to satisfy my needs. And second, I committed myself to the daily habit over the next 25 years of telling myself what I wanted. These two decisions shifted me from the frustrating world of needing and scarcity to the deeply satisfying one of wanting and abundance.

Collaborating in the creation of abundance.

This escape from competition puts the emphasis on the way you're going to grow: through cooperation, which is non-political. Instead of seeing other people as competitors for scarce resources that you need, wanting enables you to see

Wanting What You Want

> **NETWORKS OF WANTERS USE TECHNOLOGY & TEAMWORK TO COLLABORATE AND CREATE...**
>
> **ABUNDANCE!**

others as collaborators in creating greater abundance. As you move forward with this collaborative mindset, you bypass the world of politics.

In the scarcity world, cooperation like this is very temporary and begrudging. People will cooperate, but it's hard for them to do. They call it compromise rather than cooperation. Even when progress is achieved, it's not very satisfying because they achieve only some of what they need. True cooperation that is always satisfying and always expanding is possible only in the abundance world.

This shift in human affairs from scarcity-based competition to abundance-based cooperation is happening right now because of technology. In the last 20 years, the cost of communicating and collaborating with people has been

Chapter 2

brought down to almost zero. The technology and the tools that are now available to individuals for continually multiplying their own unique talents and achievements are very low-cost.

Entrepreneurs leading shift into a new world.

This is a new age of cooperation, where people are supported, enhanced, and multiplied by technology. There's been a fundamental crossover into a new world within the last two decades and it's happening first at the level of entrepreneurs.

Entrepreneurs in every industry and marketplace are the "lead dogs" of human progress. Their individual achievements make it possible for everyone else to achieve in ways that are bigger and better. They are the forward scouts for the rest of humanity, and this is because they commit themselves at an early stage of their lives to strive for freedom rather than security.

Entrepreneurs, more than everyone else, are motivated by their internal ambition rather than by outside competition. And, therefore, compared to the global population, entrepreneurs are the ones who are least constrained and burdened by energy-draining political competition.

Politics entails compromising to get what you need. It's attached to the idea that not everyone gets what they need, which is true. With need, you have to negotiate with other people's needs: "Who can help me fill the need? Who is preventing me from filling the need?" This means you get only some of what you need, so you're always lacking.

Bypassing needing, scarcity, and politics.

The act of wanting is non-political. You simply *create* in your mind what you want to create in the world through greater cooperation that is immediately available. You free everyone else up from the responsibility of satisfying your needs. This bypasses negotiation, approval, and acceptance. You focus on inventing new structures and processes to create what you want. Since wanting bypasses needing, it also bypasses the political activity that takes up many people's lives and uses up much of their lifetime energy.

My own experience since 1978 has convinced me that the increasing activity of wanting creates a lifetime of expanding freedom and a daily experience of creativity and cooperation that bypasses all political competition.

Chapter 3:
Transformation: Gaining The Capability

The person who's operating from a position of need will not know that they are. This is true of 99 percent of people on the planet. Talking to them about their needing is like talking to a fish about water. They've never been in any other environment. Their knowledge about life is all about needing. Their attitudes are entirely about needing, as are their skills and habits. And the older someone is, the harder it can be to change. So the question is, can someone who has been a lifetime needer switch to being a wanter?

Yes. It takes just two initial adjustments to get started. The first adjustment can happen for you in the next 60 seconds. This is the trigger that allows people to see why wanting is so much better than needing. Here it is: Someone who's always been in the needing mode can immediately change to being a wanter if they can grasp one thing. It has to do with a single word: *justification*.

The biggest change is to just stop justifying.

When you're in the world of needing, you always have to justify what you need because the needing world is one of scarcity. If you need something scarce, you have to rationalize why you should have it rather than someone else. Not only do you have to justify what you need to yourself, but you have to justify it to everyone else as well. Someone who is a lifetime needer spends a great deal of daily thinking and communication in a never-ending process of justification.

But if you cross the line and go into the world of wanting, there's no justification. Ever.

Wanting What You Want

MOST PEOPLE HAVE NEVER KNOWN ANYTHING OTHER THAN NEEDING, SO THEY **AREN'T EVEN AWARE THAT THEY'RE DOING IT.**

DID YOU EVER THINK OF GETTING OUT OF THE WATER?

OF COURSE I--

WAIT, GO BACK... **WATER?**

NEEDING | **WANTING**
JUSTIFICATION | NO JUSTIFICATION

WELL, YOU SEE, I NEED THIS BECAUSE...

I COME FROM...

I'M NOT VERY...

SORRY!

AND I FEEL BAD THAT...

I ONLY ASK SINCE...

SORRY!

THE REASON YOU WANT IT IS **BECAUSE YOU WANT IT!**

Chapter 3

The reason why you want something is because you want it. Period.

When I say this to successful entrepreneurs, it's an enormous, life-changing relief to them. In a matter of a minute, a huge burden can be permanently lifted from their minds. What I tell them is this: "You're free from justification as long as you're coming from a position of wanting." So right now, if you're in the needing world, you absolutely have to justify what you need because, by definition, you're taking something scarce from somebody else who also needs it. In the wanting world, however, you didn't take anything from anyone else. In the wanting world, there is an abundance of resources as a result of the creativity and innovation that come from wanting.

Taking a stand and never going back.

There's a stand entrepreneurs have to take to not give in to their previous need to justify. Some courage is required here. You have to be committed to living in a world of wanting and not falling back into a life of needing. When somebody asks you, "Why do you need that?" (because they'll say *need* rather than *want*), there's a temptation to slip back into previous language and begin to justify. You mustn't give in to that. Say, "First of all, I don't need it; I want it." And then, "The reason I want it is because I want it."

This is not easily understood by everyone because, for most people, everything in their needing world has to have a justifying reason. When you're dealing with scarcity, you probably are taking someone else's scarce resource. But in the world of wanting, there's no scarcity, because it's a world of innovation—not of taking. Wanters are creating things that

> ONCE YOU STOP JUSTIFYING YOURSELF AND BECOME A *WANTER*, YOU START TO PROGRESS THROUGH A SERIES OF **GROWTH STAGES.**
>
> 10% 25% 50% 80%
>
> HUGE CAPABILITY

didn't exist before. You're creating something new that in no way requires taking something from someone else.

Crossing over from one world to another.

Learning to want creates a crossover from the world of scarcity to the world of abundance. It's like you're going from a black and white world to a world of color. Like going from a world of single-source sound to a world of surround sound. It's a qualitatively different world.

This transformation, moving from needing to wanting, is a capability. The more you do it, the better you get at it. Yes, it's a risk at first because your previous tendencies of justification are well developed and habitual. This will be a real departure from your previous life. But I assure you, you'll get better at it as you do it over and over again.

Becoming a wanter through a series of jumps.
After you commit to quit justifying, the second adjustment is to become a wanter through a series of growth stages. You might start off at 10 percent wanting and 90 percent needing. Then you go along and you're at 25 percent wanting and 75 percent needing. Then you go along further and you're 50/50. It takes time because it has to be acted out in the real, practical world. It's not enough to just want to want. You have to work on it.

Every time you make progress in the direction of greater wanting, you experience a jump in personal confidence. There is an immediate sense of expanded freedom. You feel lighter, more energized, and more optimistic because you have just reduced the burden of justification.

A future bigger and better than the past.
Your capability for wanting will grow stronger with increased use. The more you practice successful wanting, the more powerful your skill of wanting will become. It grows your opportunities. It grows your resources. It grows your results. As you become a more powerful wanter, this capability also makes your future increasingly bigger and better than your past. With your increased capability of wanting, you speed up your personal progress. You can get what you want. Your wanting capability develops many new and greater by-products and bypasses the world of needs where most other people spend their entire lives.

You don't need anyone's approval or permission.
As I moved through my 25-year project of writing what I wanted in my daily journals, only a few people knew about this until I was near the finish line. When I reached the end

of 2003, everything in my life had transformed for the better. And never once during that quarter-century of personal transformation did I ever ask anyone else's permission to want what I wanted. Never once did I feel any need to justify what I wanted or to justify any of the dramatic progress I was making.

So, remember, you don't need anyone else's approval, permission, or support to do this. Wanting is a permanently *independent* capability that doesn't have anything to do with what others need. It is completely free of the need for justification.

Chapter 4:
Letting Go Of "Giving Back"

One of the things I often notice is that a lot of entrepreneurs who are very successful don't feel good about their success. They feel they need to justify it because, in their minds, their success somehow takes away success other people could have had. It's almost like there is only so much success in the world, and they feel they are asking for more than their share. Therefore, they have to justify it to the people who aren't as successful.

So there's a lot of guilt in the entrepreneurial world. Successful people are guilted into giving their time and money to others who didn't accomplish as much. A message is sent to them saying, "OK, you've taken so much from society. Now start giving something back."

"Needers" have the idea that there was only so much success available in the world, and you took yours and now you have to share some of it with others. This is on entrepreneurs' minds all the time if they come from a needing perspective.

"Giving back" undermines further success.
You can break it down to the point that it's impossible to say what it is that you took that you're now obligated to give back. After a while, it discourages people from achieving any greater success or creating anything new because it seems like every act of creativity increases a social debt you have. It becomes a disincentive.

These successful entrepreneurs are actually the creators of the new jobs, the creators of new breakthrough methods, but they have a strong feeling that somehow there's a huge

THE IMPERATIVE TO
GIVE BACK!
UNDERMINES FURTHER
CREATIVITY & SUCCESS
THE "NEEDERS" BELIEVE THERE'S ONLY SO MUCH SUCCESS IN THE WORLD -- SO YOU'D BETTER NOT TAKE MORE THAN YOUR FAIR SHARE!
ABUNDANCE
"GIVING BACK" DISCOURAGES FURTHER ENTREPRENEURIAL AMBITION, CREATIVITY, & SUCCESS.
GUILT

payment they owe society, that there's a huge recompense they're going to have to undertake as a result of this success.

It actually drives some entrepreneurs a bit crazy when I talk with them about this. They'll say, "Look, I've lived my life based upon justification and you've just said that the wonderful skill of justifying I've developed all my life I can't use anymore." They get very defensive about it. It's almost like they got to the top of the ladder and I'm telling them the ladder was leaning against the wrong wall.

Creating things that never existed before.

But I'm very confident about what I'm talking about here. When people stop spending their energies on justifying what they want, they free themselves up to focus on creativity and innovation. They begin to create things that never existed before. This creativity is internally generated, which is why really great innovators always catch people by surprise.

Steve Jobs is a great role model for this. Steve Jobs never did a focus group in his life. He was totally opposed to focus groups. He said that all a focus group would tell him is what they need. But he wasn't interested in what they needed. What he wanted to create was something that, after it was created, people wanted it. So what generally happens with individuals who want things is that they create new things in the world.

It's also worth noting that Steve Jobs never put any emphasis on "giving back" his time and money to society to justify his great success. When asked about this, he said that he and the Apple team created beautiful technologies that mil-

> **WHEN YOU STOP SPENDING YOUR ENERGY JUSTIFYING, YOU RISE TO NEW LEVELS OF CREATIVE ABILITY.**
>
> INNOVATION
>
> JUSTIFICATION

lions of people love using and that his company created tens of thousands of jobs and billions in tax revenues. None of this would have happened if his time, attention, talents, and resources had been focused on other people's needs.

Ignoring problems, focusing on new capabilities.

In a practical sense, entrepreneurs create new products, new services, and new experiences that other people, until they came into contact with them, never knew they wanted.

Henry Ford said, "If I'd have asked my customers what they wanted, they would have told me, 'A faster horse.'" But that's what they needed—it's not really what they wanted because they didn't know what they wanted. These great innovators like Jobs and Ford didn't justify what they wanted. They created what they wanted and transformed the world around them.

There are so many great examples of people who created new things in the world that others were then able to enjoy and use. But my belief is that nobody ever created something new because they were operating out of need. They created something new because they were operating out of a sense of want.

Great innovators first innovate for themselves.

In other words, it was something that had to be dreamed up. You see, wanting is not about solving problems. Wanting is about creating new capabilities. Great innovators are always creating great new capabilities because they first wanted the capabilities for themselves.

I think that the greatest problem-solvers are people who didn't really care whether the problem was solved except for themselves. And this is not very satisfying to a lot people who want to see heroes as people who sacrifice themselves for others. But wanters don't sacrifice themselves for anything. It's not about sacrifice; it's about expansion. They are not giving up anything at all. They are actually adding and multiplying.

When people are operating from need, they can't create anything new—they can only react and compete in their existing situation of scarcity. So they turn to politics rather than to innovation, and end up with more scarcity. Each of us, therefore, can only create new, better, and different things in the world when we're operating from a place of want, when we're first expanding our own freedom and abundance.

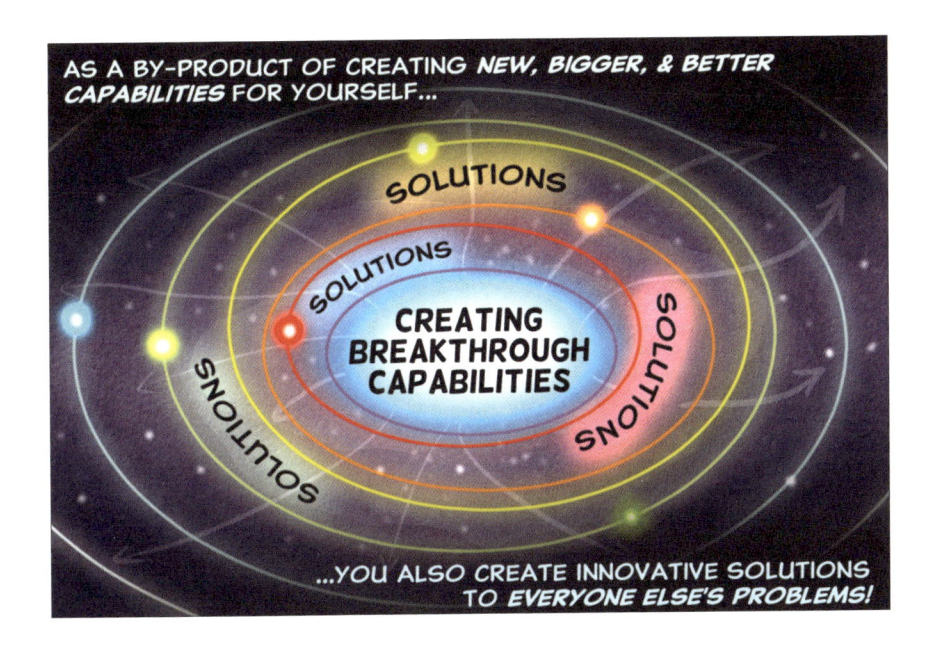

> AS A BY-PRODUCT OF CREATING *NEW, BIGGER, & BETTER CAPABILITIES* FOR YOURSELF...
>
> SOLUTIONS — **CREATING BREAKTHROUGH CAPABILITIES**
>
> ...YOU ALSO CREATE INNOVATIVE SOLUTIONS TO *EVERYONE ELSE'S PROBLEMS!*

Solving problems is a secondary by-product.

Innovators and inventors are creating new "freedom capabilities" first and foremost for themselves. They want to see something new become real and useful in the world—for themselves. The fact that their innovations and inventions subsequently solve other people's problems is an incidental and secondary by-product.

Wanters are not motivated to solve other people's problems; rather, they use them as inspiration to create something entirely new in the world that is superior to any capability that already exists. But they do this for themselves because they "want it" and because they "want *to*." This activity expands their personal sense of freedom, and, in the process, increases the general freedom of many others far more than any problem-solving can ever do.

Chapter 5:
The Four Freedoms

From our experience at Strategic Coach® of coaching more than 16,000 successful entrepreneurs over the past 25 years, we have learned a great deal about how freedom gets created and expanded in these individuals' lives. We also understand why a great many other people in today's world habitually miss out on the excitement, happiness, and satisfaction that freedom produces.

People who are needers require greater security, while those who are wanters desire greater freedom. These are two radically different motivations, and they lead to totally different and unequal results. It's like comparing life on two different planets, with different gravitational systems, in totally different solar systems. In the first world, the need for greater security actually diminishes the possibility for personal freedom. In the other, the growing lifetime desire for freedom increases the best and most permanent kind of security.

Three fundamental rules and four freedoms.

Those who are wanters increasingly understand the extra bonus they receive by focusing on freedom. They know that there are three fundamental rules for continually expanding their freedom:

1. What you want is always more expanded freedom.
2. You want these freedoms because you want them.
3. There is no justification required for any of this.

And these entrepreneurial wanters also know that there are four fundamental freedoms that are the lifetime foundation of every other kind of daily freedom: Freedom of Time, Freedom of Money, Freedom of Relationship, and Freedom of Purpose.

Wanting What You Want

FOR MORE THAN 25 YEARS, WE'VE BEEN LEARNING HOW ENTREPRENEURS *EXPAND THEIR FREEDOM.*

PLAN PLAN PLAN

RESULT!

NEEDING & WANTING ARE LIKE *TWO DIFFERENT PLANETS*:

ONE WHERE EVERYTHING IS *HEAVY*...

...AND ONE WHERE EVERYTHING IS *LIGHT*.

CHECKLIST

1. WHAT YOU WANT IS ALWAYS MORE EXPANDED FREEDOM.

2. YOU WANT THESE FREEDOMS BECAUSE YOU WANT THEM.

3. NO JUSTIFICATION IS REQUIRED FOR ANY OF THIS.

The Realm of Expanded Freedom

Freedom of Time

This first freedom refers to being able to arrange your time the way you want, both in your work and in your personal life. We have an ability as human beings to actually expand both the quantity and the quality of time in every area of daily life. Expanding your freedom of time is the starting point for expanding the other three freedoms.

Freedom of Money

The second freedom means not having an upper limit on how much money you can earn, save, and invest. And it's the individuals who are increasingly skillful with time who also enjoy an expansion of their freedom of money. Furthermore, you can use your greater freedom of money to purchase still greater freedom of time.

So, now you have two freedom tools, both of them the result of simply wanting what you want. Remember, you don't have to justify wanting and achieving either of these freedoms. You have a "wanting" tool called Freedom of Time and you have another called Freedom of Money. If you put those two freedoms together, you can now generate a third freedom, Freedom of Relationship.

Freedom of Relationship

Relationship, from the moment we are born until we die, is a constant feature of everybody's life. It's our human environment. Everything that we do and achieve occurs within our own unique world of relationships. This third freedom means you get to relate on a daily basis at work and outside of work with those you truly want to have in your life.

And when you have freedom of time and money, you can

Wanting What You Want

A UNIVERSE OF FREEDOMS SURROUNDS EVERYONE WHO CHOOSES WANTING:
PURPOSE • RELATIONSHIP • MONEY • TIME

again increase both the quantity and quality of relationships that are directly supportive of your personal purpose. And so, all of a sudden, you can see exponential growth of freedom because you're combining things that essentially multiply each other. Time multiplies money. Time and money multiply relationship.

Freedom of Purpose

The fourth is Freedom of Purpose where you can focus all of your activities on your own purposes rather than on other people's. You create your own goals and vision of how you want things to be.

All four of the freedoms expand and multiply one another. A universe of integrated freedoms surrounds, supports, and propels the forward progress of everyone who chooses wanting over needing. This is very obvious to anyone who is on this path, and very difficult to explain to those who aren't. What this comes down to then is that the expansion of freedom is its own purpose.

Needers gain freedom without earning it.

There has been a general increase of freedom, certainly in our part of the world, compared to 25 years ago. With regard to Freedom of Time, I think people generally get more time than they used to—they have shorter work hours, and more holidays have been added to the calendar. But it's the impact of time-saving technology that has been the most profound.

The majority of people, however, experience this expanding freedom in a general sense. They don't get big jumps on a personal, individual level; they get them on a general level. The same is true with money. People have more purchasing power now than they did 25 years ago. You can buy more with an hour of your work time today than you could 25 years ago. And people have more freedom to design their relationships than they did 25 years ago. There's also more opportunity to be what you want in life.

So the needing world is getting the benefits of the wanting world. They didn't get those extra freedoms because they created them. It's kind of like a gift they get, a by-product of the wanting world. They didn't do anything to earn these extra freedoms, but they get them anyway. And all of these extra freedoms for the needers of the world are actually created by a very small number of people who are wanters.

> A FEW *"WANTING PIONEERS"* TRAILBLAZE THE FUTURE THAT EVERYBODY ELSE GETS TO ENJOY & BENEFIT FROM.

Creating practical goals, activities, and results.

Wanters create their own material, physical images of what their four greater freedoms of time, money, relationship, and purpose look like. These are daily, tangible goals. And these goals lead to practical activities and results. For the most part, all of these physical and material components of their expanding freedoms are continually being created in unique ways—without any regard to competing with anyone else. Wanters tend to be increasingly oblivious to what needers are striving for. This is because nothing in the world of needing is relevant or useful for creating greater freedom.

Chapter 6:
Wanting Is About Cooperation

The world of need is characterized by intense competition, and the world of want is characterized by extraordinary cooperation. Wanting creates an expanding cooperative world because you know what you do extraordinarily well and you can see what other people do extraordinarily well. Other people's talents become increasingly valuable to you, and all you have to do is work out the grounds of practical cooperation with them.

Case study: The Two-Week Book Service.

I'll give you an example of this using the book you're reading right now. For years, entrepreneurs in Strategic Coach have told me that they're working on writing a book. I would ask them, "How long have you been working on this book?" and they'd usually reply, "I've spent the last four or five years pulling together some notes." I would say, "How are the notes going to become a book?" and the reply was always, "I don't really know how that's going to actually happen yet."

I've heard this over and over. They all have the same story. If I talk to 100 clients, maybe one of them has a book written. And for those who have the book, it was a very painful experience. It might have taken two or three years to get it out of them.

Yet, at Strategic Coach, we have a rule when it comes to creating our own books. Generally speaking, start to finish, we're going to turn out the book within about 90 days, from first idea to finished copy—a book in hand. We just found a way to work it out. The book you're reading is one example of this.

Wanting What You Want

WANTING CREATES AN EXPANDING WORLD OF COOPERATION

FOR EXAMPLE...

MANY OF MY CLIENTS WANT TO WRITE A BOOK

BUT ALL THEY HAVE IS *YEARS & YEARS* OF NOTES.

SO I'VE GIVEN THEM A FORM THAT LETS THEM *STRUCTURE A WHOLE BOOK* IN JUST A *HALF HOUR.*

THE IMPACT FILTER

MY CLIENT *DEAN JACKSON* SAID:

HEY, I COULD MAKE A *BUSINESS* OUT OF THIS!

90MINUTEBOOK.COM

NOW, I COULD HAVE TAKEN PEOPLE THROUGH THIS PROCESS, BUT THAT'S NOT WHAT WE DO.

SO INSTEAD OF *COMPETING* WITH DEAN, I GLADLY *COOPERATE* WITH HIM...

IMPACT FILTER — INTERVIEW — TRANSCRIPT WRITING FORMATTING COVER PRINTING — BOOK

...KNOWING THAT THE CLIENTS I SEND HIM WILL HAVE A FIRST DRAFT OF THEIR BOOK IN JUST *TWO WEEKS.*

Chapter 6

I showed the entrepreneurs in my workshops how, by just using a form we call The Impact Filter™, they could actually structure a book in about a half hour. Then, using the completed Impact Filter, somebody else could write the book for them or collaborate with them to write it.

At one point, we considered offering this service to our clients. Then my client Dean Jackson came along and said, "I bet I can produce a business out of this." Instead of feeling competitive toward him, I said, "Dean, if you can produce it, I'll just take all the people in Strategic Coach who are interested in this and say, 'Get in touch with Dean, go through the process, and you'll have your book, just like that.'"

Even though I was already showing clients a process that would allow them to create a book in a short amount of time, publishing their books wasn't the kind of thing we really wanted to do in Strategic Coach. So the fact that Dean now offers this capability, where I can just cooperate with him and send clients to him, works out perfectly. And clients can get a first version of their book back in two weeks.

Helping others expands my capability.
The fact that my entrepreneurs can come back with a book in a short period of time is a great benefit to me in Strategic Coach. It takes a huge chasm they used to fear crossing, this two- or three-year ordeal they used to face in publishing a book, and reduces it to a very pleasant process. As you can see, in the world of wanting, what falls away is the competition with other people. I'm not in competition with others, but rather on the lookout for teaming up with other people like Dean Jackson who are wanters.

Wanting What You Want

CONNECTING WITH THE UNIQUE GENIUS OF OTHER WANTERS *EXPANDS YOUR CAPABILITY.*

GENIUS

CAPABILITY

The world of needing becomes an increasingly competitive activity, but it's just the opposite in the world of wanting where everything becomes incredibly cooperative. In this world, someone else's wanting something is a real inspiration to me. There is this enormous supportiveness that I experience. When I live my life in a wanting mode, and I come across another wanter, I notice that I'm really inspired.

Every wanter has a unique genius.

In my world, everybody is developing their genius in some area. And you can't compete with someone else's genius because it belongs to them. When you're working in your area of Unique Ability®—what you love to do and do best—and focused on creating what you want, any idea of competition is made obsolete. And you understand that there is so much more to be gained through collaboration with other creators.

The five invisible rewards.

In the world of needing, getting rewarded for your work usually means only one thing: money. But in the world of cooperative wanting, I've discovered that there are five additional "invisible" rewards, each of which can be more valuable than money. Here's how these rewards came from my cooperation with Dean Jackson.

Capability: By encouraging Dean and his team to develop the "fast book" service for our Strategic Coach clients, I also acquired this new capability for myself and used it to create the first draft of this book in two weeks. At the same time, more than a hundred entrepreneurs have now published books using Dean's process, and many more will be able to do so in the future.

Creativity: Because I was able to obtain the first draft so quickly, I've been able to include the work of Hamish MacDonald, a cartoonist, to support the ideas. And his work, in turn, inspired ways for me to improve the copy in the final version.

Credibility: Word has spread quickly about my cooperation with Dean Jackson, and the fact that Dean keeps all of the money from the process reinforces my reputation of being useful in any way I can.

Connections: Dean, who has always been a big supporter of Strategic Coach, has increased the number of referrals he makes to my Program. At the same time, many of the new authors who used the process have acknowledged the value of Strategic Coach in their books, which have been distributed to tens of thousands of other potential Strategic Coach clients.

> IN THE WORLD OF COOPERATIVE WANTING, THERE ARE FIVE *INVISIBLE REWARDS* BEYOND MONEY:
>
> INVISIBLE REWARDS
>
> CAPABILITY
> CREATIVITY
> CREDIBILITY
> CONNECTIONS
> CONFIDENCE

Confidence: The fact that I have created so much productive activity for hundreds of entrepreneurs simply by cooperating with Dean now makes me confident that I can do this with many other individuals with valuable capabilities.

This cooperation came about because of my wanting all of my Strategic Coach clients to have the great book publishing service that Dean Jackson has created. I didn't have to spend any time or money to do this, but because of my cooperative approach, I now have a great capability for myself and others that keeps getting better for everyone involved.

Chapter 7:
Wanting Is Energizing

When you look at the mindset, activity, and results of wanting, they're not exhausting or draining. It's actually the opposite. You're adding something new to the world, focused on the future and on creating, which is energizing.

Mindset: You realize that you're using your own imagination and thinking skills to create a bigger and better future for yourself. Every time you want and achieve something new, your confidence that you can do this for the rest of your life keeps growing. And as you get older, you keep getting better at doing this. This is an incredibly energizing way of thinking about everything in your life.

Activity: You immediately take constructive and productive action without asking for anyone else's approval, permission, or support. Knowing that you can achieve everything you want, and knowing that your ability to do this keeps improving, is extraordinarily energizing.

Results: Something entirely new keeps being created in your life, which takes other people completely by surprise. Even more energizing is the fact that you keep surprising yourself with innovations and inventions that are superior in entirely new ways. No matter how good things are for you right now, you know that in the future they will always be even better.

Needing others' energy drains energy.
People who are needy don't create their own energy, so they try to get it from other people. The more energy they take, the greater their needs become. Improvement keeps getting harder and more exhausting.

Wanting What You Want

MINDSET   ACTIVITY   RESULTS

PERPETUAL ENERGY MULTIPLIER

MINDSET
GETTING BETTER & BETTER AT CREATING A BIGGER FUTURE.

ACTIVITY
TAKING ACTION WITHOUT ASKING FOR APPROVAL -- & KNOWING YOU CAN ACHIEVE WHAT YOU WANT.

RESULTS
WOW.

CONSTANTLY SURPRISING YOURSELF & OTHERS WITH WHAT YOU CAN CREATE.

People who are always tired complain about a lack of energy. Everything they do wears them out. There may be medical reasons for this, but in many cases the lack of energy stems from their "needing" approach to daily situations. Their mindset that other people should provide what they need is energy-draining. The way they act with other people only compounds the problem. And the results they get only make things worse.

On the other hand, when you want something, you create your own energy. As you get better at wanting, your energy keeps growing to the degree that you commit yourself to a path of achieving what you want. And being a skillful wanter keeps attracting more energy and keeps creating more energy for others around you. Imagine wanting greater capabilities, resources, and opportunities—and always moving forward to achieve them. This energizing activity completely bypasses the world of energy-draining needers.

Eliminating justification works wonders.

When you make the transformation from being a needer to being a wanter, you will immediately stop justifying wanting what you want. This is a huge shift in your life and it's impossible to overestimate the change that takes place in your personal energy. It's like a light switch instantly illuminating a dark room. All of a sudden, you recognize that all the energy you were spending on justification comes back in the form of creativity, innovation, and cooperation. It's like you had been using 80 percent of your daily energy for justification and that entire amount of energy comes back. Once you can make that switch from the justification model to the innovation model, it's wonderful, because now you have an endless source of self-generating energy.

Avoiding every kind of wasteful competition.

Competition for scarce resources is probably one of the most wasteful forms of energy on the planet. This is what every needer in the world is doing. It's easy to see how and where this is happening in the world around you. It shows up in every form of envy, jealousy, resentment, and outrage that consume many people's daily thinking and activity. And it can be about anything that people perceive as scarce and feel they're not getting their share of. Anytime someone is complaining or criticizing instead of creating and cooperating, you can be sure that they're trapped in some form of wasteful competition. Instead of just focusing on their own purpose and expanding their freedoms, people use up all their energy and become totally reactive. Virtually all the negative emotions we have are tied up with competing in the needing world.

The joy of focusing on your own purposes.

There's a phrase, "Mind your own business," that works perfectly here. You can say that in the world of needing, people continually deprive themselves of energy because they're minding everyone else's business while neglecting their own. And what they want other people to focus on are their needs. Instead of taking responsibility for their own progress and well being, they have an expectation that other people should being doing this. And, of course, when others fail to take care of them and their needs, they lose energy.

From the description above, it's pretty easy to see what the solution is that will turn this around. Start minding your own business! This means focusing on what you really want, which also means that you free up everyone else in the world from the responsibility of satisfying your needs. There's a joy that comes from this because you let go of unrealistic expectations about what others should be doing for you.

When you free others up, you immediately experience your own energizing freedom to create whatever you want. You immediately get back all the energy that was previously devoted to minding other people's business. This happens instantaneously because it's essentially the greatest attitudinal shift you can make in your entire life.

Energy-gaining vs. energy-draining.

After having conversations about this with my entrepreneurial clients in their Strategic Coach workshops, I found that they would come up to me the next quarter and say, "I can't tell you how much that conversation we had in the last workshop warned me about how energy-draining needing could be and how much energy has been freed up for me in not having to justify what I want. I don't have to do that anymore."

The great American psychologist William James had a crucial observation in the 1890s that predicted what is increasingly possible for everyone here in the 21st century: "The greatest discovery of my generation is that a human being can alter his life by altering his attitudes."

Every attitude related to the wanting world generates energy, while attitudes related to the needing world drain energy. Each of us can make a life-changing shift to an energizing world with a change of attitude.

Chapter 8:
Wanting Is Rewarding

I ended Chapter 6 by listing the five "invisible rewards" wanters receive when they increase their cooperation with other wanters. Here, I'll explain these rewards in more detail.

1. Others' capabilities as your opportunities.

By cooperating with others instead of competing against them, and by observing what they're creating with their unique capabilities, you also gain new capabilities.

Everyone today is increasingly surrounded by the results of other people's wanting, and it shows up in new capabilities that are useful for our own expansion of freedom. But you have to be a wanter to see other people's capabilities as your opportunities. If you're a needer, it's likely that you'll see their capabilities as competition.

If we go back to the four defining characteristics of the needing word—security, external, scarcity, and reactivity—you can see that none of them leads to an alertness about new opportunities.

On the other hand, every one of the factors involved in the wanting world is rewarding: This world is about freedom, and freedom is rewarding. The fact that wanting is internally generated is rewarding. The fact that it is abundant and creative is rewarding.

2. More cooperation equals more creativity.

In gaining a new capability, your creative skills are going to increase because you can use this new capability to transform your existing skills and achievements.

Wanting What You Want

REWARD Nº1 — CAPABILITIES

REWARD Nº2 — CREATIVITY

REWARD Nº3 — CREDIBILITY

Chapter 8

When you cross the border from needing to wanting, you notice that your brain starts working differently in a remarkable way. You begin to see that other people's creativity in expanding their freedom rubs off on you in your approach to everything in your daily life.

As you observe what they're doing, you use their improvements to creatively upgrade all of your own capabilities and achievements, and you quickly realize that there is no end to doing this. As you look at the lifetime ahead of you, everything is more exciting and motivating because you know that every time you expand your cooperation, you will be rewarded with your own greater creativity.

3. Growing credibility as a great cooperator.

With the success of your cooperation with others, it's going to be widely known that you were an important part of their success, which will lead to more credibility. Having a reputation as a cooperative rather than competitive person has five major advantages:

People see you as a source of opportunity rather than as a threat.

You are included in exciting new projects.

People find it easy to say great things about you.

Your life becomes increasingly friction-free.

Others are motivated to imitate your approach.

If you visualize each of these five advantages continually

REWARD №4

expanding and reinforcing one another out into the future ahead of you, it's easy to see why everything in your life will become increasingly abundant. And, even more important, it's easy to see why you'll be naturally motivated to improve your reputation and credibility as a great cooperator who helps everyone else to increase their personal freedom in their future.

4. Great connections are always being made.

Your increasingly successful collaborations will lead to all sorts of connections with other people you wouldn't have met under any other circumstances.

When you look at the five advantages listed above, it's easy to understand why greater cooperation leads to new, exciting, and surprising connections. Remember that most people

Chapter 8

are still trapped in the needing world where competition rules daily life. The normal experience for them is that cooperation related to anything new is something that takes a lot of work and effort. So it comes as a great shock when they encounter someone whose whole approach to life is to cooperate in the expansion of everyone's freedom. What happens is that the news about such an unusual person spreads rapidly and widely and attracts others who are also motivated to cooperate. And this is how new creative, productive, and profitable connections are made all around the world.

5. Confidence about a breakthrough future.

As you continue to be a part of the wanting world, your overall confidence as a creator and as a wanter is going to increase. You will keep involving yourself in bigger cooperative endeavors that produce bigger and better results for others—and for yourself.

This is a wonderful world I'm describing here, but it's not some idealistic fantasy that might or might not happen sometime in the future—it's actually happening in the world around us.

As a coach to highly successful entrepreneurs for over 40 years, I continually ask the individuals I work with about their experiences when they know they were wanting rather than needing. In every case, they become excited about the energizing freedom they remember. And what they remember is that they were cooperating rather than competing and that every time they've cooperated in this fashion, it led to entirely new and surprising connections that opened the door to breakthroughs. What I notice most about these "rememberings" is that they equip our Strategic

REWARD Nº5

Coach entrepreneurs with increased confidence about how they're going to approach their future.

This whole book has been about the contrast between the two dramatically different worlds of needing and wanting. My own personal conclusion after more than 70 years of testing and experience is that choosing the latter world is a no-brainer. I've spent years in the needing world, and it involved mostly pain and very little gain. Since I made the switch to the "wanting what I want" world, it's been all about increasing excitement and reward. My goal now is to pass on what I've observed and learned to as many other freedom-seeking individuals as I can who can move to an entirely new world in the very short time it takes to read this book.

Conclusion:
A Lifetime State Of Play

I started this book by recounting the events of August 1978 that prompted me to make two decisions to turn my life around:

1. Free everyone else up, in my mind, from responsibility for my welfare and success.

2. Every day, write down in a journal what I want, and do this for the next 25 years.

Happy childhood of freedom and abundance.

Looking back on the results of these two decisions, I realize that following through on both of them has actually returned my mindset to what it had been when I was a playful six-year-old. This is significant because my mother had commented to me once that she thought I was the happiest child she had ever known.

When I think about what she said, I know that I was happy way back then in the 1940s and 50s because I was a born wanter and not a needer. I also think that this is true for a great many other children—they start off as natural wanters with an expanding sense of freedom and abundance, and then for one reason or another, lose track of this experience as they get older.

In my own case, I can see now how I got off my happy track in my twenties and thirties through a series of bad attitudes that were reinforced by bad decisions and habits. It's very clear to me now that there was a 15-year period during which my thinking was increasingly trapped in a mindset of needing, where I was looking at things from a perspective of external demands, security, scarcity, and reactivity. This was happen-

Wanting What You Want

EXPANDING SENSE OF FREEDOM

BAD ATTITUDES = BAD DECISIONS = BAD HABITS

Conclusion

ing in both my personal and work life, and to me that explains why I ended up both divorced and bankrupt.

I recount this lesson because the question arises: *In addition to making the two adjustments I described earlier, what's the fastest way for people in the needing world to make the shift to the world of wanting?* My best answer is that they need to get back in touch with their childhood selves.

Entrepreneurs just doing what they want to do.

An important characteristic I've noticed about entrepreneurial wanters and creators is that they tend to have a childlike quality. When I watch them working and listen to how they describe their lives, I find it's a lot like my memories of building sand castles on the beach.

They're just doing what they're doing because their minds thought up something new. This ability to play as children is our training for wanting. When you're being playful, you're in a world of wanting. But when it's not play, it's a world of needing.

As a child, you have an abundance of things that you can do with your time and endless creativity. Entrepreneurs retain that feeling of abundance and freedom.

Entrepreneurism isn't just a sub-category of the economic world. It's actually the global role model of what's possible for all human beings on the planet. The constant activity of entrepreneurs, the enlarging of their ambitions, the increase of their productivity, and the multiplying of their results and achievements is an enormous contribution to everybody in society—everybody's welfare goes up as a result of what entrepreneurs do.

ENTREPRENEURIAL WANTING HAS THE SAME FOUR CHARACTERISTICS AS CHILDHOOD PLAY:

INTERNAL — FREE — ABUNDANT — CREATIVE

Teaching everyone how to play.

Entrepreneurs are actually the great teachers and role models for how other people can live their lives. If you were to study the great creative entrepreneurs and identify their knowledge, attitudes, skills, and habits, I think the resulting lessons would be the foundation for the number-one school for humanity during the 21st century.

If you live in the modern world, you've had the experience of needing. But to the degree that you've been able to play as a child, you've already had the experience of what it means to live in the world of wanting.

One of the things that you notice with a lot of individuals is that, as they get older, they have mastered all the habits and attitudes of needing, but they've lost the ability to play.

There is no play in their lives. I believe the reasons people are told to stop playing and start being an adult all have to do with scarcity. It all has to do with the needs world.

What differentiates entrepreneurs and wanters from others is that from a very early age, they experienced the contrast between the needs world and the wanting world and they said, "I'm going to put all my bets on wanting and escape from the world of needing." At that juncture, their lives separated from their families, from the kids they grew up with at school, and they went into this other world—a world of play. A world of creativity and abundance. A world of freedom.

Taking entire responsibility for yourself.

It's important to note that it's unlikely I could have had this conversation about the distinction between needs and wants 25 years ago, and I was probably more in touch with other entrepreneurs then than anyone else was. Indeed, this conversation has emerged right now because of a fundamental technological transformation in the world. The technological world is at the cutting edge of everybody's wanting. It's actually the outward form of the collective wanting of the planet.

Wanting is a major lifetime capability. Some people are very good at wanting, and those who aren't end up with a lifetime of needing. Above every consideration, the key to being a skillful wanter is the recognition that this is entirely a personal choice. Nobody can force you to want anything. Other people can force you to need many things, but when it comes to wanting something in the future, it is entirely a matter of personal choice. What it comes down to is your ability to imagine a bigger and better future—and then to make the decisions

PERSONAL CHOICE

DEPENDENCY | RESPONSIBILITY

and take the actions to make it into a practical reality.

When you take the wanting approach to your future, it also means that you're leaving behind the world of needing. It means that no one else is responsible for your future progress and success. You are taking on the entire responsibility for telling yourself what you want in every situation and in every circumstance. This is not easy to do at the beginning, but it is easy to understand once you start. And the more you understand that a "wanting future" is increasingly superior to a "needing future," the easier it will be to go in this direction.

And, finally, for my part, I now realize that August 15, 1978 has turned out to be one of the happiest days of my life.

The Strategic Coach® Program
Expanding Entrepreneurial Freedom

Through my decades of coaching successful entrepreneurs, and through my own personal experience, I know that entrepreneurs require concepts, structures, and processes to keep them on track with this wanting approach to life. Even more importantly, they need a permanently expanding community of like-minded teamwork where other people are also committed to expanding their freedom.

An expanding community of freedom-focused teamwork.

A community that's committed to creative wanting gives you the encouragement and inspiration to increase your wanting capabilities, opportunities, and results. If the community you're in right now doesn't give you this kind of support and energy, it's time to switch to a new one.

Strategic Coach is the only entrepreneurial community in the world with the single focus of expanding each individual's freedom and then multiplying it through accelerating teamwork with other successful, talented, and ambitious wanters. All of this freedom-focused teamwork is established and developed on an integrated platform of wanting-based concepts and tools that have been tested and refined through the practical experience of more than 16,000 entrepreneurs over the past 25 years.

The entire Strategic Coach Program, from the moment you join, is about expanding your personal entrepreneurial freedom. Your world can become a world of "wanting what you want" rather than of needing. This way, you can become as successful as you want to be rather than satisfied with being as successful as you need to be.

Wanting What You Want

You don't need us, but you will want us.
You're probably already as successful as you need to be, but it's not doing the job of actually allowing you to really want what you want.

I often say, "Our best clients don't actually need us, but they want us." Our best clients already know how to be successful by the world's standards—they're at the top—but there is something they'd like to get free of, and that's having to justify wanting what they want in life. What they want is to continually expand their four freedoms of time, money, relationship, and purpose within networks of increasing cooperation that multiply their five invisible rewards.

They'd like to live the rest of their lives, both business and personal, in a realm where they're doing what they want because they want to.

Proving that the world of wanting exists.
Strategic Coach exists today because my wife, Babs, and I wanted it. We are both playful people. We love our relationship together, and we didn't want to see any difference between the life we live personally and the life we live economically. I think the way in which we organize our company, the kind of relationships we have with our team members, the relationship that Babs and I have with each other, and the way we treat everyone who comes into the Strategic Coach Program is very powerful proof that this world of wanting actually exists.

Strategic Coach is a lifetime thinking process that empowers you and equips you with the tools to make your creative vision of your bigger future a reality. And you get to do it in a

Wanting What You Want

community of people who are also following that same path.

There are hundreds of coaching programs for successful entrepreneurs that focus you on the world of needing. They sharpen your awareness of all the scarcities, uncertainties, marketplace threats, and unexpected competition that can undermine your security.

But if you've finally had your fill of that needing-based mindset, Strategic Coach provides the ideal place for you to switch to a completely freedom-expanding way of experiencing your entrepreneurial life.

Take action: Visit us online at *strategiccoach.com* or call us at 416.531.7399 or 1.800.387.3206.